Jesus in the Manger

LINDA WARD

Jesus loves you!

Linda M Ward

ISBN 978-1-63525-093-0 (Paperback)
ISBN 978-1-63525-094-7 (Digital)

Christian Faith Publishing, Inc.
296 Chestnut Street
Meadville, PA 16335
www.christianfaithpublishing.com

Printed in the United States of America

Dedication

This book is dedicated to my children and grandchildren, and children of all ages. My hope is that you will always seek the truth and wisdom of God's Word, and enjoy the gift of Christmas every single day.

Christmas season actually begins on Christmas Eve and lasts for twelve days, ending on January 6. The time before Christmas is commonly called Advent, or a season of preparation for Christmas. Christians celebrate this Advent season in a variety of ways that fit their religion and family traditions. During Advent, Christians often take time to prepare their hearts to celebrate our Savior's first coming to Bethlehem as an infant and to remind ourselves that Jesus is the greatest gift of Christmas. In order to prepare for Jesus's birth, we will look at each piece of the Nativity scene, how it got its place in Scripture, and the significance for us all.

We have all heard the saying, "Home Is Where the Heart Is." The first piece of the Nativity is the stable. Not many of us would choose to have our baby born in an animal shelter or barn. What is it about a stable that makes this piece of the Nativity seem so unwelcoming? A dirty floor, untidy surroundings, unsanitary conditions, no fire for warmth, no comfortable bedding—perhaps these are just some of the things that come to mind.

"In those days Caesar Augustus issued a decree that a census should be taken of the entire Roman world. So Joseph also went up from the town of Nazareth in Galilee to Judea, to Bethlehem the town of David, because he belonged to the house and line of David. He went there to register with Mary, who was pledged to be married to him and was expecting a child."

The great influx of pilgrims into Jerusalem and nearby communities like Bethlehem caused Mary and Joseph to find rest in a stable because according to Scripture, there was no room for them in the inn. (Luke 2:1-7, NIV)

It was here that the Creator of the universe would be born. He left behind almighty power and the riches of heaven in order to take a human form and be born of peasant parents. This humble birth is significant in that it tells us that he did not need the power of this world to achieve his goals. Whether it was a stable, a barn, or a cave is not clearly known from Scripture, but what we do know it was a birthing place no one would imagine for a King.

"For you know the grace of our Lord Jesus Christ, that though he was rich, yet for your sake, he became poor, so that you through his poverty might become rich." (2 Corinthians 8:9, NIV)

Yes, home is where the heart is. The very heart of God was born in a stable!

Newborn babies don't recall the first bed that their parents laid them in or where they were born. More than likely outside of a hospital crib, the bedding a new infant would be placed into would be soft, warm, and clean. By adding the manger to the Nativity scene, we are actually putting an item in place that Scripture names.

"And she gave birth to her firstborn, a son. She wrapped him in cloths and placed him in a manger." (Luke 2: 7a, NIV)

A manger, a feeding trough for animals. It is this identified item of the Nativity scene that gives us the idea that baby Jesus was born in a stable, barn or even a cave. It was a place where animals were fed.

It's no is coincidence that Jesus was placed into a feeding trough. He is the Lamb of God; he told his disciples to feed his sheep. Symbolically, the manger, the feeding trough is dirty and empty, a rather nasty place to lay a baby. In our lives before Jesus, we are dirty and empty too. The perfect Lamb of God will soon occupy this manger. He came to show his love for us, share his life with us, and give up his life for us so we can no longer be dirty and empty.

"The third time he said to him, 'Simon son of John, do you love me?' Peter was hurt because Jesus asked him the third time, 'Do you love me?' He said, 'Lord you know all things; you know that I love you.' Jesus said, 'Feed my sheep.'" (John 21:17, NIV)

The Nativity animals are not specifically described in Scripture. We do know that the trip from Nazareth to Bethlehem by foot was at least a three-day journey for Mary and Joseph. Being that Mary was very pregnant and probably could not walk the entire way, it is not hard to imagine they had a donkey, which was a typical animal used at that time for travel and transportation. It is also not hard to imagine that in this stable, there were other animals from other travelers such as Mary and Joseph, animals that would have been kept by the common folk of that time such as sheep, goats, cows, or oxen.

Our Lord often spoke of himself as a shepherd, someone who looks after his beloved flock. It would only be natural to add these humble animals to the Nativity. Their survival, their lives are in the hands of their master. Just as we should be in the hands of the Master.

"I am the good shepherd: I know my sheep and my sheep know me. Just as the Father knows me and I know the Father-and lay my life down for the sheep." (John 10: 14–15, NIV)

Mary, the mother of Jesus was the one chosen by God to have his Son. In all the Earth, it was she, a humble young girl engaged to be married to Joseph and suddenly she finds herself being visited by the angel Gabriel. The Bible's account of the announcement to Mary is found in Luke 1:26–33 (NIV): "In the sixth month of Elizabeth's pregnancy (Mary's cousin), God sent the angel Gabriel to Nazareth a town in Galilee to a virgin pledged to be married to a man named Joseph, a descendant of David. The virgins name was Mary. The angel went to her and said 'Greetings, you who are highly favored! The Lord is with you.' Mary was greatly troubled at his words and wondered what kind of greeting this might be. But the angel said to her, 'Do not be afraid, Mary; you have found favor with God. You will conceive and give birth to a son, and you are to call him Jesus. He will be great and will be called the Son of the Most High. The Lord God will give him the throne of his father David, and he will reign over Jacob's descendants forever; his kingdom will never end.'"

Clearly Mary had, even at her young age, a very mature under-standing of who God is and how important it is to be obedient to his calling. From this encounter with the angel Gabriel, Mary did not waiver in her faith. She called herself the Lord's servant. Loving God was more important to her than the possible difficulties of facing those who might question her sudden pregnancy and the explanation she would give.

Despite the fact that the angel Gabriel told Mary in Luke 1:28 (NIV) that she was highly favored by God, simply meaning she had been given much grace or unmerited favor, Mary would still suffer greatly. In time, she would one day be highly honored as the mother of the Savior, but she would first know disgrace as an unwed mother, nearly lose her betrothed husband Joseph, and her beloved son would be rejected and die a cruel death on a cross. Mary's submission to God's plan would cost her dearly, yet she was willing to be God's servant. How much are we willing to sacrifice to be God's servants?

"Through Jesus, therefore, let us continually offer to God a sacrifice of praise--the fruit of lips that openly profess his name. And do not forget to do good and to share with others, for with such sacrifices God is pleased." (Hebrews 13:15–16, NIV)

As he did with Mary, God chose Joseph, a humble righteous man to be the earthly father of Jesus. The Bible tells us in the Gospel of Matthew 1:18–19 (NIV): "This is how the birth of Jesus the Messiah came about: His mother Mary was pledged to be married to Joseph, but before they came together, she was found to be pregnant through the Holy Spirit. Because Joseph her husband was faithful to the law, and yet did not want to expose her to public disgrace, he had in mind to divorce her quietly."

His actions toward Mary revealed he was a kind and sensitive man. When Mary told Joseph she was pregnant, he certainly knew the child was not his, and Mary's apparent unfaithfulness under Jewish law meant he could divorce her and she could be stoned to death.

"But after he had considered this, an angel of the Lord appeared to him in a dream and said, 'Joseph, son of David, do not be afraid to take Mary home as your wife, because what is conceived in her is from the Holy Spirit. She will give him the name Jesus, because he will save his people from their sins.'" (Matthew 1: 20–21, NIV)

The Bible does not give much detail about Joseph's role as the earthly father to Jesus, but from Matthew 1, we see that he was an example of how integrity and righteousness would help shape the face of fatherhood in future generations. Joseph set a high standard for the role of fathers, stepparenting, adoption, and fostering children placed in their care. Joseph's integrity was honored by God. He trusted him with a great responsibility. Think of your own children when you are away from them, it's not easy to fully trust their care to someone else. Picture God looking down through the expanse of time to choose one man to raise his own son. Joseph had God's trust. What is God trusting you with?

"Whoever can be trusted with very little can also be trusted with much, and whoever is dishonest with very little will also be dishonest with much. So if you have not been trustworthy in handling worldly wealth, who will trust you with true riches?" (Luke 16: 10–11, NIV)

In modern-day times, when a baby is born, there are typically baby showers, couple showers, a baby registry, and gifts for the newborn they cannot even fathom. Clearly, times have changed since the birth of our Lord, Jesus Christ. No showers, no registry, and some unusual gifts, which will be explored later. However, the birth of our Lord was foretold, expected, and greatly anticipated. Without the clear 3-D images of who and what the baby Jesus would be, we do have scriptural references to his birth, a biblical baby shower of sorts.

"Therefore the Lord himself will give you a sign: The virgin will conceive and give birth to a son, and will call him Immanuel." (Isaiah 7:14, NIV)

"But you, Bethlehem Ephrathah, though you are small among the clans of Judah, out of you will come for me one who will be ruler over Israel, whose origins are from of old, from ancient times." (Micah 5:2, NIV)

"Of the greatness of his government and peace there will be no end. He will reign on David's throne and over his kingdom, establishing and upholding it with justice and righteousness from that time on and forever. The zeal of the Lord Almighty will accomplish this." (Isaiah 9:7, NIV)

"He will be great and will be called the Son of the Most High. The Lord God will give him the throne of his father David, and he will reign over Jacob's descendants forever; his kingdom will never end." (Luke 1:32–33, NIV)

A virgin birth in the town of Bethlehem, from the ancestry line of King David, the Son of the Most High, these are just a few fulfilled prophecies of the birth of Jesus. Only a God who loved mankind so much would give a gift so perfect and eternal, so real and personal that fits exactly right every time!

"For God so loved the world that he gave his one and only Son, that whoever believes in him shall not perish but have eternal life." (John 3:16, NIV)

Can you imagine a gift more precious than that? Welcome, baby Jesus! Merry Christmas!

When a newborn comes into the world, there is great excitement and adoration of the new baby. Phone calls are made, family and friends visit the baby, and it seems nothing is more wonderful than a beautiful newborn baby. Jesus was greatly adored by His father, and like most parents, God was excited to announce His Son's birth, but in a way that only God can do.

"And there were shepherds living out in the fields nearby, keeping watch over their flocks at night. An angel of the Lord appeared to them, and the glory of the Lord shone around them, and they were terrified. But the angel said to them, 'Do not be afraid. I bring you good news that will cause great joy for all the people. Today in the town of David a Savior has been born to you; he is the Messiah, the Lord. This will be a sign to you: You will find a baby wrapped in cloths and lying in a manger.'"(Luke 2:8–12, NIV)

25

Shepherds were the first to hear about the birth of the Messiah. Yes, shepherds, not Jewish rulers or kings, but to people who were considered to be among the lowest in social status. Again in Scripture, our Lord's birth makes mention of a manger, most likely found in a stable or animal shelter, a place that would be familiar to shepherds who were encouraged to go and find Him, which they did.

"So they hurried off and found Mary and Joseph, and the baby, who was lying in the manger. When they had seen him, they spread the word concerning what had been told them about this child, and all who heard it were amazed at what the shepherds said to them." (Luke 2:16–18, NIV)

Shepherds, people who dedicate their lives to the care and well-being of their flocks. People who must sacrifice daily comforts and companionship who might be called meek. In Matthew 5:5 (NIV), Jesus said, "Blessed are the meek, for they shall inherit the earth." Jesus himself was a shepherd of sorts, oftentimes calling himself that. He understood meekness, a humble, patient, quiet nature. Someone who is submissive to a higher authority. Generations later, we don't need the miraculous sign of a baby in a manger to be obedient to what God is calling us to be. We need to be the excited witnesses of the miracle of Jesus, and like the shepherds, we spread the word.

27

Psalm 19:1 (NIV) says, "The heavens declare the glory of God; the skies proclaim the work of His hands."

Imagine the shepherds sitting out in the fields on a beautiful starry night, admiring the heavens and the stars when suddenly, an angel appears with what could only be somewhat spectacular and terrifying at the same time. In fact, Scripture says they were terrified, and then suddenly, the skies were ablaze with God's spectacular birth announcement!

"Suddenly a great company of the heavenly host appeared with the angel, praising God and saying, 'Glory to God in the highest heaven, and on earth peace to those on whom his favor rests.' When the angels had left them and gone into heaven, the shepherds said to one another, 'Let's go to Bethlehem and see this thing that has happened, which the Lord has told us about.'" (Luke 2:13–15, NIV)

Go, see, tell. Christmas is all about letting our hearts return to the manger in Bethlehem and receive the gift from God, His precious Son, see how he changes our lives, and share this gift with others.

The final characters that are found in most Nativity sets are the wise men, or Magi, who made their visit to the new King.

"After Jesus was born in Bethlehem in Judea, during the time of King Herod, Magi from the east came to Jerusalem and asked, 'Where is the one who has been born king of the Jews? We saw his star when it rose and have come to worship him.' When King Herod heard this he was disturbed, and all Jerusalem with him. When he had called together all the people's chief priests and teachers of the law, he asked them where the Messiah was to be born. 'In Bethlehem in Judea,' they replied, 'for this is what the prophet has written: "But you, Bethlehem, in the land of Judah, are by no means least among the rulers of Judah; for out of you will come a ruler who will shepherd my people Israel."'" (Matthew 2: 1–7, NIV)

The Magi set off for Bethlehem to find the new King. Just how many "Magi" there were is not specified in Scripture, but because they brought three gifts of gold, frankincense, and myrrh, it is generally believed that there were three wise men, scholarly men who knew something of prophecy and that the star they had seen was a significant sign that they simply could not ignore. Following the star, they continued on their journey until, according to Scripture, they found the child with His mother in a house, where they worshiped Him and pre-sented Him with their gifts.

"After they had heard the king, they went on their way, and the star they had seen when it rose went ahead of them until it stopped over the place where the child was. When they saw the star, they were overjoyed. On coming to the house, they saw the child with his mother Mary, and they bowed down and worshiped him. Then they opened their treasures and presented him with gifts of gold, frankincense and myrrh." (Matthew 2: 9–11, NIV)

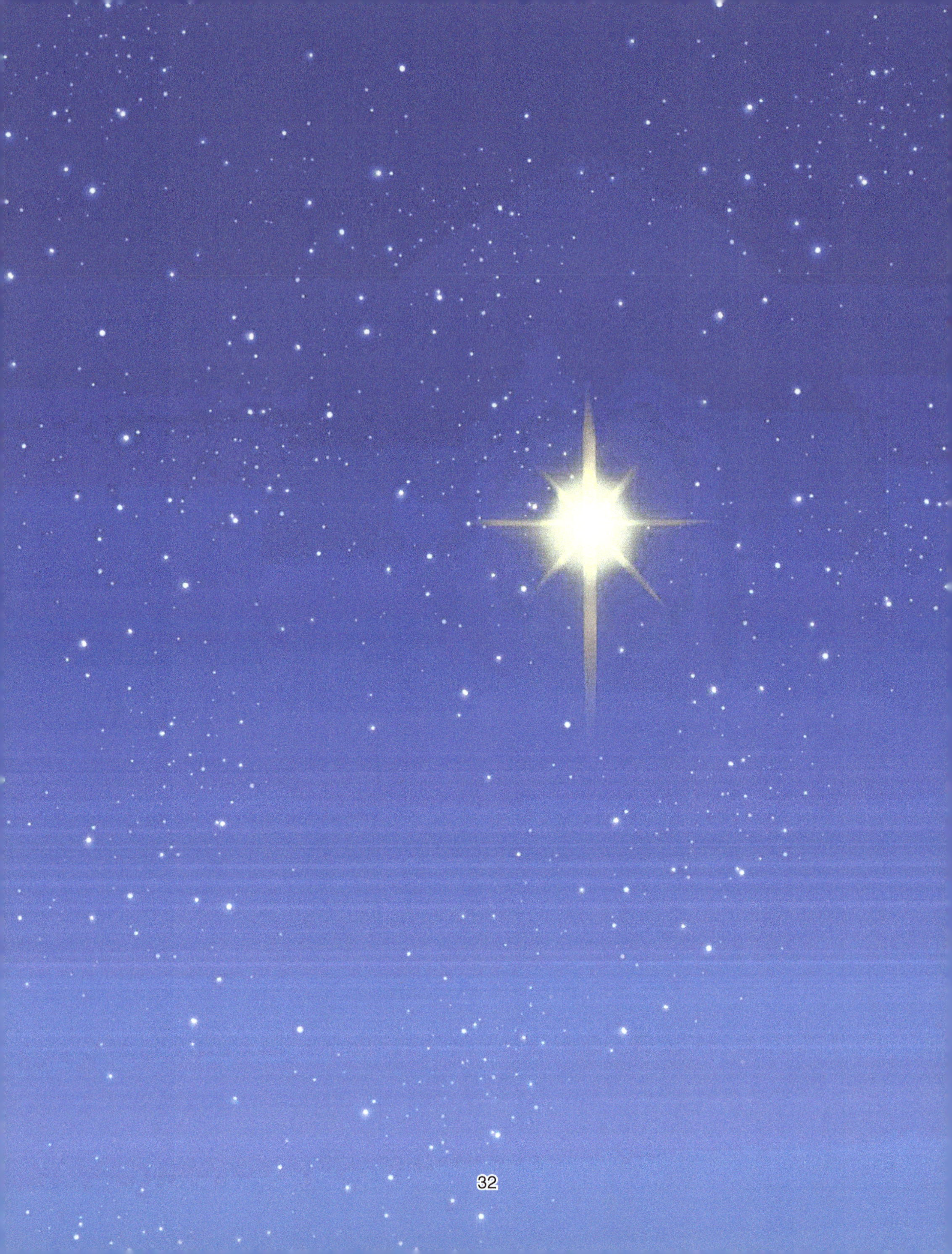

It is unclear from Scripture how old Jesus was when the Magi made their visit to Him, but they did not visit Him while He was in the manger. Adding the Magi to the Nativity brings the Christmas story of Jesus's birth to a convenient close. The Christmas pageants have been performed, Christmas Eve services are done, the gifts have been unwrapped, and the Christmas dinner has been served. In many Christian households, the end of the Christmas season ends on January 6, to commemorate the visit of the Magi, an event that happened sometime after the birth of Jesus.

January 6 is called "The Epiphany." The *Merriam-Webster Dictionary*'s definition of *epiphany* is as follows: "Epiphany; a Christian festival held on January 6 in honor of the coming of the three kings to the infant Jesus Christ." It is the secondary definition of epiphany that is far more significant to the celebration of Christmas: "a moment in which you suddenly see or understand something in a new or very clear way."

Are you following a "star"? Are you still seeking Him? Are you looking for wise men or angels to help you to have an epiphany? Take one more look at the pieces of the Nativity. Remember their significance and their roles. Recognize that God does not need you, he wants you, he seeks you!

"Where is the wise person? Where is the teacher of the law? Where is the philosopher of this age? Has not God made foolish the wisdom of the world? For since in the wisdom of God the world through its wisdom did not know him, God was pleased through the foolishness of what was preached to save those who believe. Jews demand signs and Greeks look for wisdom, but we preach Christ crucified: a stumbling block to Jews and foolishness to Gentiles, but to those whom God has called, both Jews and Greeks, Christ the power of God and the wisdom of God." (1 Corinthians 1:20–24, NIV)

Have you answered His call?

Hopefully your epiphany is that Christmas is not just a day, an event, or a celebration. It is a life of living with the gift of God, Jesus Christ, our Lord and Savior.

About the Author

Linda Ward is a retired elementary school teacher. Teaching reading was her favorite subject. She taught for twenty-three years, thirteen years in a private Christian school, and ten years in a public elementary school. She was teacher certified ASCI (Association of Christian Schools International) when in the private school and also held an educator's license for Texas public elementary schools. She also has a master's in education.

Linda is married to her best friend for life. They will celebrate thirty-four years of marriage this year. They have three grown children, two girls, and one son. Their daughters are married and have blessed them with three wonderful granddaughters to date.

Linda's hobbies are Bible studies with some of her best girlfriends, cooking, gardening, caring for their four-legged "children," and of course, traveling to see their precious ones as they all live out of the area.

Raising a family and teaching, she never really had the time to pursue her desire to someday write children's books. Now that she has the time, she feels led and encouraged by God to write for Him, about Him, and to honor Him.

Printed in the USA
CPSIA information can be obtained
at www.ICGtesting.com
CBHW081231141223
2646CB00001B/1